How Do We Generate and Use Electricity?

 HOUGHTON MIFFLIN HARCOURT

PHOTOGRAPHY CREDITS: COVER (bg) ©Hero/Corbis; 3 (t) ©Corbis, (c) ©RTimages/Alamy Images, (b) ©Fotolia XXV/Fotolia; 5 (b) ©Ocean/Corbis; 8 (b) ©Image Source/Getty Images; 9 (t) ©Mangiwau/Flickr/Getty Images; 10 (b) ©Photodisc/Getty Images; 11 (b) ©GIPhotoStock/Science Source/Photo Researchers, Inc.; 20 (b) ©Nicholas Eveleigh/Getty Images

Printed in Mexico

ISBN: 978-0-544-07316-6

2 3 4 5 6 7 8 9 10 0908 21 20 19 18 17 16 15 14 13

4500456326   A B C D E F G

Be an Active Reader!

Look at these words.

electric motor	circuit	magnet
conductor	series circuit	electromagnet
insulator	parallel circuit	generator

Look for answers to these questions.

What is electrical energy?

Which devices use electricity?

What is electric charge?

How do electric charges move?

What is static electricity?

How is a conductor different from an insulator?

What is an electric circuit?

How is a series circuit different from a parallel circuit?

How does a magnet work?

How can electricity make an electromagnet?

How does a generator produce electricity?

What is electrical energy?

What would it be like to live without electricity for one day? Without electricity, you couldn't turn on the lights. You couldn't use a computer or watch television. Electricity is electrical energy, which provides the energy for many of the things you use.

Electrical energy is produced from an electric current. Devices plugged into a wall outlet operate on the energy produced by an electric current. The energy from batteries is also electrical energy.

A light bulb gives off light because of electrical energy.

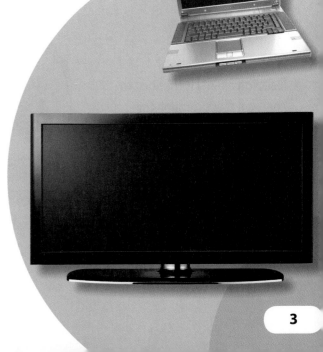

Which devices use electricity?

Did you listen to music, make toast, or ride in a car or bus to school today? If so, you used electrical energy. Electricity provides the energy for many of the devices we use every day.

Electrical energy can change into other forms of energy, including light, heat, sound, and motion. Toasters use electrical energy to produce heat. When electricity passes through wires made of certain metals, the wires get very hot and start to glow. When you turn on a toaster, electricity passes through wires inside the bread slots. These wires are made up of loops. The wire loops heat up, giving off enough heat to toast the bread.

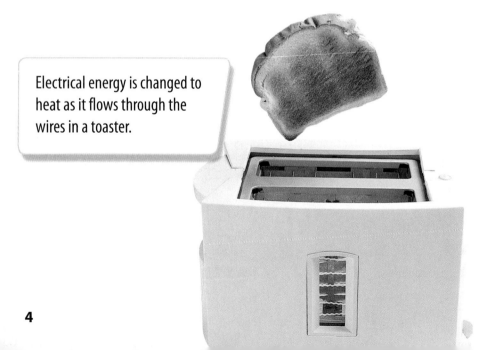

Electrical energy is changed to heat as it flows through the wires in a toaster.

A smartphone changes electrical energy into light and sound. When you turn on a smartphone, you see pictures and hear sounds. A smartphone uses a battery, but it can also be plugged into an electrical outlet. Electricity is necessary to recharge the battery.

Some electrical devices get their energy from electric motors. An electric motor is a device that changes electrical energy into motion. A remote-control toy car is moved by an electric motor. Electric motors are in many of our home devices. Washing machines, dryers, and vacuum cleaners all have electric motors.

Electricity provides energy to many of our portable devices.

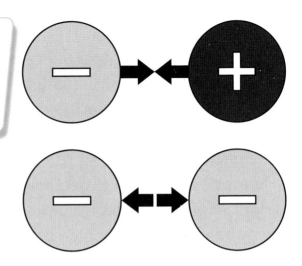

Particles with opposite charges attract each other. Particles with the same charge repel each other.

What is electric charge?

Electricity is the result of the movement of electric charges. To understand electric charge, you need to know something about atoms. Atoms are the tiny particles that make up all matter. Inside atoms are even smaller particles. Two kinds of these particles have different electric charges. Electric charge is a property that affects how a particle behaves around other particles. Some particles called protons have a positive charge. Others called electrons have a negative charge. A third kind of particle, neutrons, has no charge at all.

Positive and negative charges are opposites. A positive charge and a negative charge attract, or pull, each other. Charges that are alike do the opposite: they repel, or push each other away.

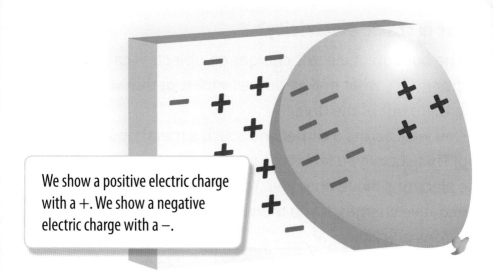

We show a positive electric charge with a +. We show a negative electric charge with a −.

How do electric charges move?

Most objects have an equal number of positive and negative charges. Therefore, the charges cancel each other out. Charges stay on an object until that object comes close to something that has a different charge. When two objects rub together, charged particles transfer from one object to the other. If you rub a balloon with a wool cloth, negative charges move from the wool to the balloon.

What happens if you hold the negatively charged balloon against a wall? The balloon sticks to the wall. This is because the negative charges of the balloon become attracted to positive charges in the wall.

What is static electricity?

The buildup of electric charges on objects is called static electricity. It's what makes clothes stick together when you take them out of the dryer.

You walk across a carpet and touch a metal doorknob. Zap! That shock you feel is the movement of electrons. The electrons move onto you. Your body gets a buildup of negative charges. If you then touch a doorknob, the electrons quickly move to the doorknob. This fast movement of electrons is called an electrostatic discharge. You feel the discharge as a small shock. Sometimes you might even see or hear the discharge.

Static electricity can literally make your hair stand up!

After static electricity builds up, it can be released as electrostatic discharge. Lightning is a form of electrostatic discharge.

Most of the time, the discharges you feel only give you a quick, tiny zap. Lightning, on the other hand, causes huge shocks, and it can be very dangerous. Lightning is a large electrostatic discharge that can occur during a storm. Inside a cloud, ice and rain droplets rub against each other. Electric charges build in the clouds. Positive charges form at the top of a cloud and on the ground. Negative charges form at the bottom of the cloud. If the buildup of charges becomes great enough, the charges can move. They can move between a cloud and the air, or between clouds. They can also move between a cloud and the ground below.

How is a conductor different from an insulator?

A flow of electric charges is called an electric current. Any material that allows electric charges to move easily through it is called a conductor. Most metals, such as copper, iron, gold, and silver, are conductors. Many of the electrical wires in our homes are made of copper. Aluminum is also a good conductor of electricity. Most electrical lines are made of aluminum.

Electric charges also flow through particles found in water. Pure water is not a conductor, but most water is not pure. It has dissolved substances that act as conductors. That is why you should never use electric devices near water or swim during an electrical storm.

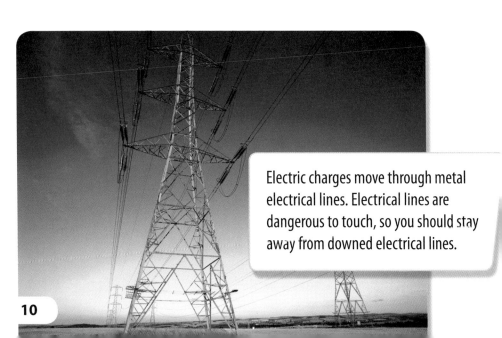

Electric charges move through metal electrical lines. Electrical lines are dangerous to touch, so you should stay away from downed electrical lines.

A material that can block the flow of electric charges is called an insulator. Most solid materials that are not metals are insulators. Rubber, glass, wood, and plastic are examples of insulators.

Conductors and insulators are used to control the flow of electric charges. An electrical cord has both conductors and an insulator to control the flow of electric charge to an appliance. Plastic and rubber are good insulators; that's why they cover most electrical cords. Electricity can flow through the wires inside the cord, but it can't flow through the plastic or rubber to shock your hand. The covering over the wires makes the electrical cord safe to touch. For the same reason, the part of the plug that you touch is also made of plastic or rubber.

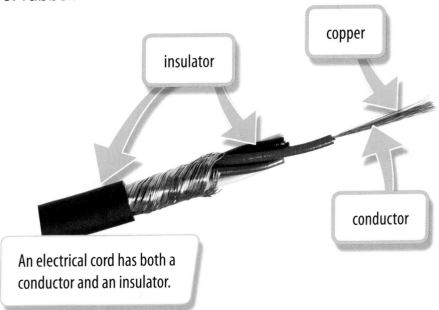

copper

insulator

conductor

An electrical cord has both a conductor and an insulator.

What is an electric circuit?

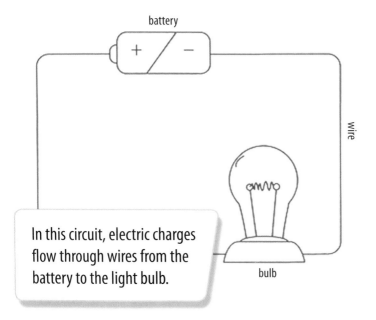

battery

wire

In this circuit, electric charges flow through wires from the battery to the light bulb.

bulb

   Electric current must flow in a path. The path along which an electric current flows is called a circuit. Look at the circuit above. This circuit has parts: an energy source, a load, and connectors. An energy source is the source of electricity that provides energy to the load. Here, the energy source is a battery. A load is any device that uses electricity. In this circuit, the load is the light bulb. Connectors are wires that carry the electric charges between the energy source and the load. For the bulb to light, the wires must connect the battery and light bulb to form a circuit. This flow of electricity is called a current.

Electricity cannot flow if there are any breaks or gaps in the circuit. A circuit with a break or gap is called an open circuit. The path in an open circuit is not complete. In this situation, the bulb will not light up. A complete circuit with no breaks or gaps is called a closed circuit. Electricity flows in a closed circuit, so the bulb will light up.

Many circuits have a switch. The switch is turned off and on to close and open a circuit. When the switch is turned off, the circuit opens. The electricity cannot flow, and the bulb goes dark. When the switch is turned on, the circuit closes, allowing the electricity to flow and the bulb to light up.

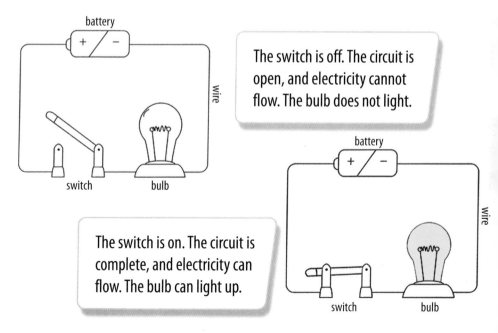

The switch is off. The circuit is open, and electricity cannot flow. The bulb does not light.

The switch is on. The circuit is complete, and electricity can flow. The bulb can light up.

How is a series circuit different from a parallel circuit?

Not all circuits are the same. A series circuit has only one path for electric charges to follow. This kind of circuit can have more than one load. Remember that a load is an electrical device, such as a light bulb.

Think about a circular train track. All the trains travel in the same direction. This is how a series circuit works. The picture below shows a series circuit. One wire connects all the parts. When the light bulbs are in place, the circuit is closed. The charges flow, and the bulbs light up. If you remove a light bulb, the circuit is open. Charges do not flow, and the bulbs do not light up.

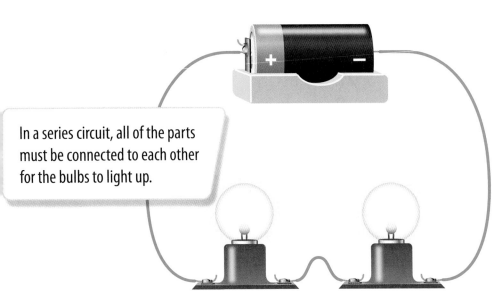

In a series circuit, all of the parts must be connected to each other for the bulbs to light up.

Imagine a train set with different tracks that all lead to the same station. This will help you to visualize what a parallel circuit is like. In a parallel circuit, charges can flow through more than one path.

In a series circuit, the same current goes through the entire path. In a parallel circuit, the current is split between the different paths. Some current flows through one path. Some flows through the other. Look at the circuit below. Both loads, or light bulbs, connect to the energy source through separate paths. If you remove one light bulb, the other will remain lit. That is because the current is still flowing through the complete circuit in the other branches.

In a parallel circuit, charges can flow through the top loop and the bottom loop. You can remove one light, and the other will still glow.

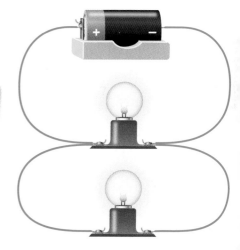

How does a magnet work?

Did you know that magnets make many things you use work? Magnets are in computers, televisions, and smartphones.

A magnet is something that attracts iron and certain other metals, such as nickel and cobalt. The attraction is called magnetism, and it is one of the physical properties of matter.

A magnet has two ends, called poles, where the magnetic force is strongest. One pole is called the north-seeking, or N, pole. The other is called the south-seeking, or S, pole. An N pole and an S pole are unlike poles, so they attract, or pull toward, each other. Two N poles or two S poles repel, or push away, each other.

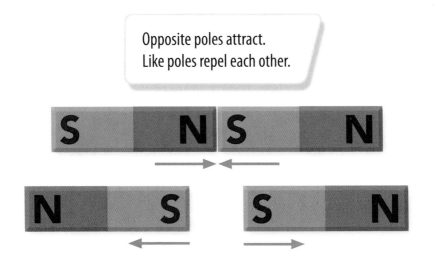

Opposite poles attract.
Like poles repel each other.

Every magnet has a magnetic field, the space around the magnet where the force of the magnet acts. You can't actually see a magnetic field. It is invisible. If you sprinkle iron filings around a magnet, though, the iron filings show the field's shape. Look at the diagram below. It shows the magnetic field around a bar magnet. The field is strongest around the *N* and *S* poles. The field is weakest in the center of the magnet.

Magnets come in many shapes and sizes. The strength of a magnet depends on its size as well as the type of material that was used to make it. Not all magnets are made by people, however. Some occur in nature. A rock called lodestone is a natural magnet.

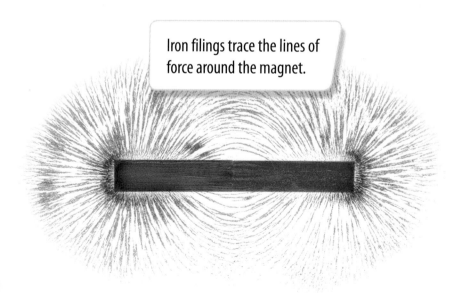

Iron filings trace the lines of force around the magnet.

How can electricity make an electromagnet?

When electric current flows, it also makes a magnetic field. This means that we can use electric current to make magnets. A magnet made by using electricity is called an electromagnet. It's possible to make an electromagnet by wrapping a wire around an iron nail, and then attaching a battery to the wire to make a closed circuit. When electricity flows through the wire, a

This electromagnet is made using a battery, connectors, and wire wrapped around a nail.

magnetic field forms around the nail. The nail then becomes a magnet that attracts objects.

The electromagnet in the photograph attracts paper clips. If you stop the current, the magnetic field will disappear. The paper clips will fall.

We rely on electromagnets every day. They are used in video games, fans, and smartphones. An electric motor is made up of a magnet and an electromagnet. An electric motor is a device that uses electricity to make things move. A magnet always attracts certain metals. An electromagnet can be on or off. When the motor is on, current flows through a wire. This turns on the electromagnet. The magnetic fields of the magnet and electromagnet interact. The two magnets push and pull on each other. These forces spin a shaft. Electrical energy changes into motion!

An electric motor uses a magnet and an electromagnet to change electrical energy into motion.

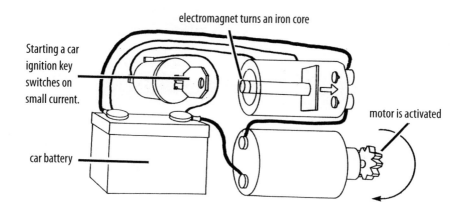

electromagnet turns an iron core

Starting a car ignition key switches on small current.

motor is activated

car battery

How does a generator produce electricity?

Machines called generators are used to produce electricity. A generator uses motion to produce electricity. A generator has many of the same parts as a motor. It has a permanent magnet, an electromagnet, an energy source, and a wire loop attached to a rod.

For a generator to work, the wire loop must be turned. The loop spins between two poles of a magnet. The magnetic field makes an electric current in the wire loop. Electric charges move through the loop when it gets close to the poles. These moving charges are the electric current.

A generator is a device that uses mechanical energy to produce electricity.

A generator needs motion to work. Where does it get the motion it needs? Hand cranks are used to start up some generators. You must turn the crank to get the motion. Most generators use a turbine. A turbine is a set of blades attached to a shaft.

Many turbines look like electric fans. Wind, water, or steam can be used to turn the blades of a turbine. The turning blades spin the shaft. The shaft spins the wire loop inside the generator. Electric current is made. Steam provides energy for most turbines. The steam is sent through a pipe pointed at the blades.

Generators in energy stations produce the electricity we use at home, work, and school.

This large generator uses water for energy to turn the turbine blades and produce electricity.

generator

turbine generator shaft

turbine

water flow

turbine blades

Identify Conductors and Insulators

Adult supervision is required for this activity. You will need a nail, a pencil, some chalk, a penny, an eraser, and a paper clip. To build a circuit, you will also need three pieces of wire, a battery, and a light bulb. Set up the wires in a circuit loop. Connect the wire between the battery and light bulb. Leave the ends of the two wires connected to the opposite end of the battery and light bulb unconnected. Touch the nail with the free ends of these two wires. If the bulb lights, the nail is a conductor. If the bulb does not light, the nail is an insulator. Record the results in a table. Repeat this process for each item.

Write a Report

Write a brief report about a scientist who made important contributions to the field of electrical energy or magnetism. Find out at least five facts about this scientist's discoveries. How does what he or she discovered impact our lives today? Present your report to the class.

Glossary

circuit [SER·kuht] A path along which electric charges can flow.

conductor [kuhn·DUK·ter] A material that allows heat or electricity to move through it easily.

electric motor [ee·LEK·trik MOHT·er] A device that changes electrical energy into mechanical energy.

electromagnet [ee·lek·troh·MAG·nit] A temporary magnet caused by an electric current.

generator [JEN·er·ayt·er] A device that makes an electric current by converting mechanical energy to electrical energy.

insulator [IN·suh·layt·er] A material that does not allow heat or electricity to move through it easily.

magnet [MAG·nit] An object that attracts iron and a few other—but not all—metals.

parallel circuit [PAIR·uh·lel SER·kit] An electric circuit that has more than one path for the electric charges to follow.

series circuit [SEER·eez SER·kit] An electric circuit in which the electrical charges have only one path to follow.